The Dental Business

A Blueprint for Success

Tools, Resources and Solutions

for Dental Practice Owners and Managers

Mary Fisher-Day

Founder and Owner, The Dental Business™

Steve & Amanda:
Thank you for
the love and support you've
given me through the years.
You're truly an inspiration and
example of success in business and
in life. You have no idea how much
you both mean to me!
With so much love -
Mary

The Dental Business

Printed by:
90-Minute Books
302 Martinique Drive
Winter Haven, FL 33884
www.90minutebooks.com

Published in the United States of America

ISBN-13: 978-0692726914
ISBN-10: 0692726918

Here's What's Inside...

Getting Started: How, When and Where 1

Understanding Insurance Participation 5

Building Professional Relationships 8

Marketing 11

Practice Overhead 17

Essential Practice Management Reports 22

Being a Good Leader 26

Human Resources and Employee Management 30

Practice Policies, Protocol and Systems 60

About Your Team 66

The Patient Experience 81

Risk Management 89

Forming an Exit Strategy 95

Recommended Resources 101

About the Author

Mary's career in dentistry has spanned more than 3 decades; she has worked as an assistant, scheduling and financial coordinator, and office manager. Early in her career, she moved a lot. Although it was tough at the time, moving often did have one benefit. Mary saw the effects of management style on practice culture, employee loyalty, Patient satisfaction and ultimately Practice Success.

Realizing a strong desire to expand her career, Mary continued her education with the study of business management. Armed with experience and knowledge of the inner workings of dental practices, she was ready to begin the next phase of her career and began working with a large dental practice management and transition company. She worked as a practice management consultant with the firm until the owner decided to focus solely on practice Transitions.

Mary founded The Dental Business™ in 2002. She and her team, of experienced dental professionals, provide Coaching services for dental teams and see quick results by providing custom solutions and management systems based on the needs of the practice.

Their ultimate goal and mission, if you will, is to see dentists and their teams enjoy going to work each day, have patients that happily refer others, worry-free time away from the office and the prosperous practice they dream of.

About this book:

Written as a guide for current and future dental practice owners and managers; this book will provide management systems, tools and resources necessary to build the foundation for a Successful Practice.

I've shared a few personal experiences as examples during a pertinent subject. Yikes, it wasn't always fun. But, I hope they will be helpful!

Getting Started: How, When and Where

If you are a recent dental school graduate and plan to own a dental practice: This entire book will be your friend. Start from the beginning, make notes, highlight where needed and mark pages for future reference. You will be glad you did!

If you currently own a dental practice, this book is for you too. You will find tools, resources and strategies that help you throughout your career.

For future, Dental Practice Owners:

Important Dos and Don'ts:

Don't buy the big dream house before you buy a dental practice.

You will be limited by your debt-to-income ratio, as to the amount of money you can borrow to buy a practice.

Live below your means and pay down as much debt as possible, prior to buying a practice.

Keep in mind, it's easier to find a house near your practice, than a practice to buy, near your house.

Prequalify for a practice loan.

This is important because you need to know how much you can borrow to start a new practice or to buy an existing practice. Your lending institution will look at your credit, experience, and production records. For this reason, it is important to keep production reports early in your career

- If you're a dentist, serving our country by providing dental care to our troops and their families. First, Thank You for your service! Second, if your future plans include owning a dental practice, it's important to keep track of your production. Keep record of the number of patients you see per day and the procedures provided. Many lending institutions will require these documents.

Branding

Naming your Dental Practice.

- Choose a name you can live with for a long time. If you're a woman, give serious thought to your professional name. Some women prefer to use their maiden name as it will never change.
- Apply to your state board for approval of the practice name before you spend money on branding.
- Speak with an attorney about the legal structure of the practice. You will protect yourself, your family and your practice in doing this.

Giving your practice personality

Choose Theme, Colors, and Style you can live with for a long time. Branding a business is expensive.

Your Logo: Should reflect your personality and carry through your brand.

- Signage: Check zoning laws prior to deciding on size, color, placement and type of signage.
- Stationery: Order after finalizing name, logo and address.
- Domain(s): Purchase domains in your name and DBA (doing business as) name. Have all domains link to your website.
- Web Presence: Hiring a website designer and host should be one of the first things you do after your practice name is approved. This is not the place to save

money. Your website is the first thing a future patient will see.

- Social Media Presence: LinkedIn, Facebook, Instagram, Snapchat, and Twitter are all great social media sources to use for business growth.

Your Required National Provider Identification Number

A National Provider Identifier (NPI) is a unique, government-issued, standard identification number for individual healthcare providers and provider organizations, such as clinics, hospitals, schools, and group practices. NPIs that specify an individual, such as a solo-practice dentist, are classified as Entity Type 1 (Individual) NPIs. NPIs that specify a dental practice organization are classified as Entity Type 2 (Organization) NPIs.

Any healthcare provider that uses electronic transactions for claims or eligibility verifications is considered a "covered entity" under the Health Insurance Portability and Accountability Act (HIPAA) standard and is required under federal law to include an NPI on electronic transactions. This definition applies regardless of whether the provider submits electronic transactions directly or via a third party, like a vendor or a clearinghouse.

Applying for Your NPI Number

Applying for an NPI is free and relatively easy. To apply through a secure, web-based process, visit the National Plan and Provider Enumeration System website. Those with valid applications should receive their NPIs via email within one to five business days. The email may go to a spam folder, so check regularly to ensure you receive the message.

During the application, you will be asked for your Provider Taxonomy Code. This is an alpha-numeric code that designates a healthcare provider's area of specialization. A list of Provider Taxonomy Codes is available on the American Dental Association® (ADA) website.

Understanding Insurance Participation

Credentialing

Your decision to participate in one or multiple PPO plans is an important one, choose your plans carefully.

If you are a participating provider, you must accept the payment schedule as set by the insurance company. *Although it's not easy, rates can be negotiated in most states.

You may want to consider hiring a professional to handle credentialing for you or visit www.ada.org to enter your professional dental credentials and prevent the need to duplicate the credentialing process. This is especially important if you plan to participate in multiple plans or own multiple practices.

A list of items you will need to become a credentialed provider:

- Copy of your State License(s)
- Copy of your Professional Insurance face sheet
- NPI Number
- Practice information
- Education information, including graduate and residency programs
- Passing dates for NBDE

You may also be asked for your:

- Hospital Affiliation information
- Basic Life Support Certification
- Medicare Number and Medicaid Number
- Advanced Cardiovascular Life Support Certification

- Basic Life Support Certification
- Copy of your Anesthesia License, if applicable
- Copy of your DEA License
- Copy of your Controlled Dangerous Substances License

The Difference Between PPO, HMO, and Capitation Plans

Providers participating in **PPO plans** are expected to accept a reduced fee. Familiarize yourself with the plans, within the plan, to determine which if any, are beneficial to your practice. You can start by running a patient by insurance company report. This report will give you a great idea of which companies insure the majority of your patients. If you need new patients, look to larger employers in your area; Determine which insurance companies these employers use to provide benefits for their employees? Do some research on these plans to see if they would be of benefit to your practice.

HMO plans are similar to PPO plans; however, most PPO plans require the patient to pay a portion of the fee as determined by the insurance plan. HMO plans typically have an agreed-upon fee for procedures, and patients are not expected to pay the difference between the doctor's fee and the insurance company's pre-determined reimbursement rate.

Capitation plans are plans in which an employer and provider agrees to a predetermined reduced rate for contracted services. Patients covered by this plan are not expected to pay the difference between the providers' normal fee and the contracted fee for the contracted services.

Indemnity insurance plans: Insurance claims are filed as a courtesy. The practice accepts payment from the insurance company. The patient is required to pay any amount of the fee not covered by their insurance plan.

Participation in **Medicaid** is an economic decision based on the location of your practice and your patient demographic. If you practice in a rural area with a low-income population, participation may be both an ethical and a financial decision. Before you sign up as a Medicaid provider, familiarize yourself with Medicaid fees for your area.

Building Professional Relationships

Dental-Specific CPA

Having a professional relationship with a dental-specific CPA (certified public accountant) makes all the difference in the world! A dental-specific CPA understands the uniqueness of a dental practice and will advise you as to the best tax structure for your business. Your accountant can help you keep an an eye on practice overhead, and advise you as to the best way to categorize accounts payable for your practice.

Having an ongoing relationship with a dental-specific CPA will discourage embezzlement as well. If you're not yet convinced, think of your dental CPA as an alarm system for your practice finances. It's a great way to scare a thief.

Attorney

Develop a relationship with an attorney; one who will become familiar with your practice and legal entity. There will be times when you need to pick up the phone or email your attorney for quick advice. There may also be occasions when you need an attorney to write a letter on your behalf.

Certified Financial Planner

Ask friends and colleagues for recommendations of a Financial Planner. You will need one sooner than you think. It's never too early to begin this relationship.

Dental Laboratory

You will need to work with a dental laboratory for removable and fixed prosthodontics, even if you have CadCam technology. Ask for references from colleagues. When interviewing the lab, ask for a written fee schedule, the name of the provider of their metal work as well as the name of the person or company that fabricates their crowns, bridges, partials, dentures, etc. It's important that you know this information.

Dental Supply Company

Having a good relationship with a merchandise sales rep is beneficial to a practice owner/dentist and manager in a variety of ways. Your clinical supply sales rep can save you money and make your life easier by setting up OSHA (Occupational Safety and Health Administration) training and keeping you up-to-speed on the latest compliance issues. Your dental supply specialist can advise you on the latest in dental materials and technology and coordinate training on new equipment purchased through their company.

Your supply sales rep may help you find an emergency fill-in employee or provider if the need arises. He/She can provide free continuing-education courses for you as well. Today, dental sales reps are trained to do a whole lot more than sell cotton rolls. I strongly suggest you make these folks your friends.

Bank

Form a good relationship with someone in the loan department or higher at your bank. Maintaining a line of credit can be beneficial in case of emergency. The office could flood; the compressor may break or burn up; the air conditioning or heating unit may break. You never know what will happen, and it's best to be prepared.

Payroll Company

There are many payroll companies that would love to have your business. In addition, some accountants and most large banks offer payroll services.

I highly recommend that you have someone take this task off your hands. It is a waste of your valuable time. Trust me, you'll be very glad you did!

Insurance Broker

You will be required to have variety of insurance policies during your career. Having a relationship with an insurance specialist who knows the basics of the dental industry and what policies are needed, will make your life easier. Examples of insurance policies you will need include disability, overhead, life, liability, malpractice, health, and loan insurance.

Find a Mentor

It's helpful to have someone you look up to and who you would like to emulate in your practice. This type of relationship can be invaluable. Be a good student, don't waste your time or theirs, and be willing to give back or pay it forward.

Transition Consultant

If you haven't already do so, form a relationship someone who has their finger on the pulse of the dental practice transition industry. This may make no sense to you, if you're in the early years of your career. Believe me, life will throw you curve balls and you never know when you may need to, have-to or want to sell your dental practice.

Marketing

Internal Marketing

- One of the most effective ways of internal marketing is to simply ask for referrals. Example: "Mrs. Clark, we love seeing you and wish we had more patients just like you. Please refer your family and friends to us. We would love to be their dental care provider." You can tweak this verbiage any way you like. Try it and track it. It works.
- Post-op phone calls are the best internal marketing there is. It really is, if the right person makes the call. Make your own post-op phone calls if at all possible. It will take two minutes of your time, and patients will love you and refer everyone they know to you! If the dentist cannot make post op phone calls, the clinical assistant involved in the procedure should make it. Hygienists should make calls to any patient receiving Soft tissue management treatment or a difficult prophy. If a general surgeon or plastic surgeon can take the time to call their patients, shouldn't you? Your patients are important too. It's not necessary to call every patient; just patients who were nervous, had a crown prep, root canal, RPS, extraction or other procedure that was time-consuming and a little tougher than a typical filling.
- See patients at their appointed time. If you must make them wait, apologize as soon as possible. If the dentist cannot make the apology, the clinical team member that brings the patient back should make the apology.
- Unless your patient is wearing head phones, Involve patients in your conversation. They can hear you and most likely do not appreciate being ignored while you have discussions among yourselves.

Personal Story

"While having eye surgery, I listened as my surgeon and his assistant discussed office politics. They spoke about one of the partners in the practice and an employee he favored. It was very personal and unprofessional and made me extremely uncomfortable.

As you can imagine, I have since started seeing a different ophthalmologist."

Internal Marketing Continued...

- Patients should be greeted promptly and with a smile when they enter your practice.
- When speaking with a patient in your treatment room, sit down with them and look them in the eye. This simple gesture immediately instills trust. Patients accept treatment more readily from a dentist they trust. Whatever you do, please do not stand above patients when you speak with them. You will come across as impatient and uninterested. Knee to knee and eye to eye is the best way communicate with your patients.

External Marketing

There is a plethora of ways to market your practice. Following are some examples.

Postcards: These can be sent out by demographic. There are many companies that assist with postcard campaigns.

Billboards: Some like this method of advertising, and some do not. It does work.

Radio: Radio ads can be useful, but only if you can get a good deal. It's best to use a media buyer to assist with this. See more on this below

Television: Television spots are expensive, but they can be effective. If you go this route, consider hiring a media buyer to represent you. Their job is to make sure your ads or commercials are broadcast at the best time and on the best stations for your practice demographic.

Community involvement: There are a number of ways to get involved in your community. Adopt a road or highway, sponsor a local sports team, join the chamber of commerce, join civic organizations, position yourself as a 'team dentist', sponsor a local welcome wagon or ask for suggestions from your team.

Newsletter: A newsletter is usually placed on your website or sent via email each month. You can program your patient communication software to send the newsletter at the same time each month. Use Constant Contact®, Icontact, or a similar communication system or utilize a Social Media company to do it for you.

Ads in local magazines or newspapers: Place public service announcements in a newspaper or local magazine. This will educate potential patients and acquaint them with your practice

Website

Your website should be simple and easy to read, yet personal and engaging.

Most practices will need the following sections. separated by tabs.

- *About Us: This should introduce the doctor(s) and team. A picture of the Doctor and bio should headline this sections. A picture of the entire team together makes a good impression on new patients. In addition, you may ask each team member to write a paragraph about their position and how he/she will interact with patients. The paragraph should be upbeat and welcoming. This is not the place, for your team, to share personal information about their lives. Save personal information for Social Media.*

Example

Cindy, Schedule Coordinator

"Hi, I'm Cindy, and I will be the first face you see when you walk in the door. I look forward to meeting you! Please let me know if you have questions about our office. I'm here to help."

Website tabs continued...

- Our Services: List of services offered. Be sure to highlight anything you offer that other practices in your area do not.
- Testimonials: What patients are saying about you. You can transfer reviews from Demandforce®, Lighthouse360®, Solution reach Yelp, Yahoo, etc. This will link back to your review forum building your credibility and web presence.
- Patient Forms: These should include all new-patient information, health history forms, practice insurance policy, financial policy, and HIPAA forms.
- Contact Us: Include a map to the office, a picture of the practice, a form to fill out to request a call or an appointment, a phone number, and an office email address.
- Blog or Newsletter: If you have a newsletter or write a blog, you should post each one on your website. Potential patients love seeing a glimpse in to the practice philosophy and culture.

Social Media

You should have a Facebook presence and consider a Twitter account, a LinkedIn page, and an Instagram account. If you don't, you're missing out on a huge opportunity to build your practice reputation and attract new patients. These are free social media sites and all accounts can be accessed through Hootsuite. Hootsuite is a once and done program that ties all of your social media accounts together and allows you to schedule posts as far out as you like and post to all of your social media sites at once.

Update your Facebook page at least weekly with interesting and useful information. You can schedule posts months in advance. Be sure to share personal pictures of you and your team doing everyday things from time to time. This will give patients a glimpse in to your life and a sense of knowing you, which is a huge draw for new patients.

There are businesses whose sole purpose is to assist practices with social media accounts. Check out Banyan or My Social Practice. They provide great, up to date, content and photos.

Practice Overhead

Your practice overhead numbers will be found on your profit and Loss report. This report can be generated through Quick books or you may ask your accountant to provide one. In either case, it's essential to review your profit and loss report each month.

In today's dental practice culture, it's very difficult to have financial success if practice overhead expenses are too high.

There are required expenses in every dental practice. It's imperative that you keep an eye on these numbers and include your team in discussions and goals. *Including your team will make it easier to meet your objective.

Healthy overhead expenses range between 50% and 60% in a General dental practice. Specialty practice will have healthy overhead expenses between 40% and 55%.

Being aware of these numbers and take needed steps to keep them in line, will make all the difference in your practice sales price, when you're ready to or need to sell your practice.

Overhead percentages can be found in your profit and loss report. You may receive one monthly from your accountant. You can also run a profit and loss report on your Quickbooks® software. Whichever you choose, the financial health of your practice depends on your keeping track of these numbers.

Healthy Overhead Percentages by Category for a General Dental Practice:

- Employee overhead (does not including associate dentists): 24% to 26% is optimum. It's acceptable to see up to 28% for a well tenured staff. Employee overhead Includes payroll taxes and all benefits.
- Lab fees: 7% to 10% without CadCam technology. 3% to 5% with CadCam technology.

- Clinical supplies: 6% to 7%
- Office supplies: 1% to 2%
- Lease or rent: 4% to 5%
- Miscellaneous fees, such as repairs and maintenance, equipment, utilities, insurance, and professional fees in total should be 10% or less.

How to Set Up QuickBooks®

Set up your office QuickBooks® as soon as you have a business banking account, and link your account to QuickBooks®.

Below is an example of QuickBooks® for a dental practice:

Income/Expense

- Deposits (may split categories i.e. Checks, Visa, MC)
- Patient refunds

Expenses

Staff expenses and wages

- Wages and Salaries
- Fed/state payroll taxes
- 401(k) or other retirement contribution
- Health insurance for employees
- Employee meals for meetings
- Uniforms
- Temporary employees

Rent, Utilities, and Office Expenses

- Rent, mortgage, or lease payment
- Business Telephone
- Utilities
- Janitorial or cleaning
- Office liability insurance

Laboratory Fees

- C&B, removable, and orthodontics

Dental Supplies (clinical)

- Supply house(s)

Equipment

- New equipment
- Equipment lease
- Equipment maintenance
- Facility repair and maintenance fees

Marketing

- Stationery, business cards, brochures
- Online marketing (Facebook, Google AdWords, etc.)
- Gifts
- Sponsorship
- Donations
- Website design, hosting, and maintenance

- Ads

Legal and Professional

- Accountant
- Attorney
- Consultant

Other Business Expenses

- Continuing education
- Travel for business
- Malpractice insurance
- Dues and subscriptions
- Licenses and permits

Office Supplies

- Postage
- Staples
- Printing
- Subscriptions

Bank Charges

- Credit card charges
- Care credit
- Bank fees
- Interest expense

Net Ordinary Income

Other Income/Expenses:

Owner's salaries and compensation

- Wages
- Insurance
- Uniforms
- Membership dues
- Owner's taxes
- Travel Expenses
- Owner compensation – other
- Dr.'s cell phone
- Dining

Automobile

- Auto payment
- Fuel
- Mileage for patient emergency care

Payroll tax expense owner

Net Other Income

Net Income owner.

Essential Practice Management Reports

These are the reports that will help you stay on top of your practice numbers. You cannot have a healthy dental practice without monitoring these numbers.

- **Daily deposit:** This report should be run at the end of each day and compared to the end-of-day report for accuracy.
- **End-of-day:** This report should be processed at the end of each day, after deposit reports are run. The dentist, practice owner, or office manager should review this report for accuracy. The report must match the deposit report and any deposits on hand.
- **End-of-month:** This report should be run after you close out the last work day of the month. It's important that it be completed prior to the start of the first day of the following month.
- **End-of-year:** This report should be run after the last work day of the year is closed out and the month is closed out. It should include a full A/R (accounts receivable) report, production by provider and procedure report, adjustments by category report, and the production/collections report sheet.
- **Accounts receivable:** This report should be reviewed monthly and should be run as part of the end-of-month report. Less than 12% of your A/R should be over 90 days.
- **Recall:** This report should contain information on patients who are not on the schedule and have not been seen for re-care in seven months or more. The recall report should be run monthly and worked daily unless your hygiene department is booked solid.
- **Delinquent accounts:** The delinquent account report will show you which accounts are outstanding, when

payments were last made on the accounts, and whether the payments were made by insurance or patients. This report should run weekly and be worked daily.

- **Outstanding insurance or insurance tracking:** The outstanding insurance report will show you any claims that are unpaid, the dates of service, and the dates the claims were filed. Use this report to determine whether a claim needs to be refiled. The report should be run weekly and worked daily, if possible, but at least worked weekly.
- **Adjustment report:** The adjustment report should be run monthly with the end-of-month report. The report should show adjustments by type and adjustment report credits, write-offs, and discounts given to patient balances. The practice owner or office manager should approve all write offs on patient accounts and should thoroughly review the report each month. Become very familiar with this report; it's easy to read and very important.
- **New patients:** The new-patient report should be run monthly. Track your new patients to see where they come from and if they followed through with needed treatment.
- **Patient analysis:** The patient analysis report will show the number of patients you have on record, the number of patients who are active, how many patients are scheduled for re-care, how many patients are past due for re-care, the gender and age breakdown of your patient base, what percentage of your patients have insurance, and the top 10 zip codes of your patient base. This report should be run and reviewed quarterly.
- **Production by provider and procedure:** This report breaks down production procedures by provider. In reviewing it, you will see what procedures are provided

most often and what procedures are lacking. It is a huge resource for your practice.

- **Treatment plan:** This report will show you what has fallen through the cracks and what patients and procedures have not been scheduled. It's a great resource when filling gaps in your schedule.
- **Delinquent accounts:** The delinquent account report should be run monthly and worked weekly. I suggest that patients with overdue balances be contacted when they have not made payments on accounts in over 30 days. If they go 90 days without making a payment, they should be turned over to your collection company.
- **Accounts receivable report:** Your A/R report is an important report to review monthly. You need to closely monitor any account that is over 60 days past due. Make sure your financial coordinator is actively working with the patient to clear the outstanding balance.

Many Dental Practice Owners Don't Get This:

It's important to understand that your team will never be as invested in the profitability of your practice as you. Their names are not on the door or the mortgage and for the most part, their pay checks do not depend on your profitability. For this reason and many others, you should be aware of what is going on in your practice. I am not advocating micro-management. I am suggesting that you at least glance over your practice reports daily. Review monthly reports with your administrative team at minimum, and review quarterly or, at the very least, yearly reports with your entire team.

You would be shocked at the amount of money that walks out of practice doors each day because practice owners or managers who do not review daily practice reports. It's your practice. Your license and the financial well-being of your family is on the line and if you're the owner, your name is on the door. The buck stops with you.

"You are the only person who is ultimately responsible for the success of your practice." ~MFD

Being a Good Leader

First Rule: Lead by example.

- If you want your team to care about your practice, you have to show that you care. Consistently coming in to work late is akin to holding up a flashing neon sign to your staff, that says "I'm checked out and just going through the motions." Don't be that boss; be their leader, and you'll be much more successful in the long run.
- If you're truly checked out and going through the motions, sell the practice and work as an associate dentist. You won't have to worry about running a business. You can do what you went to dental school to do: practice dentistry.
- Don't flirt with an employee. Even a little flirting is not okay. It sets a bad precedence and sends the wrong message, in addition to setting you up for sexual harassment lawsuit.
- Dating a member of your team is never a good idea. Other team members will pick up on it, they always do, and they won't like it. At the very least it will be a difficult relationship. What happens when it doesn't work out? Do you fire the employee? Employers who break this rule rarely come out unscathed. The employee doesn't fare well in these situations either. Feelings will be hurt, jobs and income will be affected and in some cases it can ruin your career. It's a no-win situation. Avoid it at all costs.

*Regardless of how angry you are, there is never an excuse to discipline a member of your team in front of a patient or other team members. If you do, it will come back to bite you on the butt and will look like a jerk. You will likely lose the patient and any potential patients they would have referred. You may lose the team member as well.

In addition, losing your cool in front of your team will result in their losing respect for you. It's wrong and in poor taste. You don't want to be "that" boss!

We all have moments of anger and frustration. Part of being a good boss and leader is maintaining composure and doing the right thing, even when you want to scream.

Personal Story

My first job as a dental assistant was in a practice that was part of the clinical rotation I was required to complete while in school. I was warned against accepting this job, but Dental assisting jobs were not easy to find at the time so I accepted it. I was barely 19 years old.

The practice was large, and the dentist quite intimidating. He had a bad temper and threw instruments when things didn't go his way. He knew I was intimidated by him and loved it.

One afternoon after all of the patients were gone, I was standing at the autoclave when I felt someone behind me. Before I had time to turn around, he put his arms around me and his hands in inappropriate places. I was shocked and turned around to push him away, and he responded by placing his mouth over, what felt like, my entire face. I pushed him away and ran to the restroom. I left as soon as I heard him leave and cried the entire drive home.

I didn't tell my parents. I was too embarrassed and if I'm honest, I was afraid they would wonder if I did something to make him think his behavior was okay. Otherwise, why would a grown, married Man behave like that. Trust me, I had those thoughts. "What did I do to make him think touching me would be okay?" As I look back now, I know it wasn't anything I said or did.

I soon found another job. But that memory of my first job, still gives me a sick feeling, more than 30 years later.

"People may forget what you say or what you do, but they never forget how you make them feel." ~Maya Angelou

A Great Boss!

Because I moved a lot, during the early years of my career, I had several bosses. It's funny how the really bad and the really good ones, stand out.

My favorite boss ever practiced in South Carolina. He always had positive things to say to build his employees up, and his faith in us made us want to work harder.

He didn't hesitate to tell us when we messed up, but he would also let us know that we were appreciated. I loved my job so much and even though I drove an hour each way to work in his office, if we had not moved away for my husband's work, I would never have left.

My life would probably be very different now though and because I moved away, someone else was lucky enough to have him as their boss!

Sometimes all it takes is a Thank you! He said it often!

Human Resources and Employee Management

Unless your practice has an Office Manager, the owner or dentist will normally be responsible for all things employee-related.

Sample Job Descriptions:

Scheduling and Financial/Insurance Coordinator (Referred to as SC and FC)

The business/front office will need a scheduling/financial/insurance coordinator. The person(s) responsible for these positions must be diplomatic hostesses, housekeepers, business managers, and executive secretaries to the doctors.

The job belongs to all positions if there is nothing else noted. Depending on the size of your practice, you may have one person wear all three hats, or you may have a different person for each job title. (Job descriptions are very beneficial.)

If you have a small practice, it's important that at least two team members be trained to perform all administrative duties. This will enable your practice to run efficiently when a key person is sick or on vacation.

At the minimum, the cross-trained employee should have the ability to professionally answer phones per practice protocol, schedule patients per practice protocol, answer basic questions about and file insurance for patients (if your practice files insurance), check patients in, enter new patient information in practice management software, update health history, explain new-patient forms, and check patients out.

Basic duties are as follows:

- Greet patients upon arrival.
- Update patient records.
- Announce the arrivals of patients.
- (SC) Confirm appointments.
- (SC) Fill openings in schedule.
- (SC) Call patients to check on their status when they are 10 minutes late for their appointments.
- (SC) Maintain recall system.
- Sort incoming mail.
- (FC) Receive and record all patient payments.
- (FC) File Insurance claims, check on patient benefits, and make necessary changes to patient record.
- (FC) File pre-treatment estimates.
- (FC) Send statements.
- Handle office correspondence and filing.
- (FC) Balance books at the end of the day, month, and year.
- (FC) Run deposit, and back up computer.
- Stock and order business office supplies.
- Pull and file patient charts (if not paperless).
- Answer phones.
- Shred old documents as needed.
- Purge patient records.

Dental Hygienist

General dental practices need at least one registered dental hygienist, who has the role of clinician and teacher. Their duties include, but are not limited to, the following:

- Participate in morning huddle, and review the schedule for the day.
- Review patient records, and become familiar with patient histories.
- Remove plaque, stain, and tartar in a comfortable manner.
- Educate patients on proper oral hygiene techniques.
- Recognize periodontal disease, and inform patients of its correlation with overall health.
- Expose and develop dental radiographs as necessary.
- Place pit and fissure sealants.
- Utilize intraoral camera and patient-education software.
- Document treatment delivered and treatment recommended in patient record.
- Educate patients on restorative procedures when appropriate.
- Stock treatment room, as needed.
- Sterilize instruments.

Hygiene Production Goals: Hygiene daily goals should be determined by your fee schedule and the number patient hours available each day. As a rule, 50% of hygiene patients will need BWX, 1/3 of hygiene patients will need a panoramic X-ray or FMX and, on average, 1 perio SRP or perio maintenance per day. To determine the percentage of child prophy appointments necessary, review the patient analysis report to see the patient mix. Incorporate as indicated by the numbers. If this report is not available; a good rule of thumb is ¼ to 1/3 of a general dental practice patient base consists of children. You will likely have a good feel as to which percentage to use.

Assisted Hygiene: Utilizing a hygiene assistant is an option when you have a waiting list for hygiene appointments, an energetic hygienist, and a motivated DA I.

The assistant will seat the patient; take needed radiographs; update the medical history; and prepare the patient for the hygienist to probe, clean, floss, and polish the patient's teeth.

When the hygienist is performing the prophylaxis, the hygiene assistant will seat the next patient and repeat the process. The assistant should return to the hygiene room during the dentist's exam to take thorough notes, schedule the patient's next recall appointment, and escort the patient to the front desk to review needed treatment with the scheduling coordinator.

The scheduling coordinator will schedule the treatment at a convenient time for the patient. The hygiene assistant will return to the treatment room to clean it and then seat the next patient.

This process will allow the hygienist to see an average of five more adult recall patients per day.

How much education should a Hygiene Assistant have?

At the very least, a hygiene assistant must have passed an X-ray certification course, a CPR course and have all compliance training.

How do you schedule hygiene patients for assisted hygiene?

It's best to schedule the second patient of the day, 30 minutes after the first patient and stagger the patients from there, depending, of course, on how much time is required per patient.

If you do not need a full-time hygiene assistant, you may combine the roll with that of a clinical assistant or floater.

Clinical Assistant and Coordinator

The role of a Clinical Assistant is the most versatile roll in the office. The Clinical Assistant may assist chairside and assist in hygiene.

Their main job is to be aware of the schedule at all times and to make sure everything is running smoothly in the clinical area.

The Clinical Assistant/Coordinator should have the ability to prioritize and multi-task and should do their job with very little direction after the training period.

Other duties include, but are not limited to, the following:

- Attend morning huddle.
- Stock hygiene treatment rooms with floss, prophy cups, prophy paste, patient napkins, suction tubes, toothbrushes, gloves, plastic chair covers, and gauze.
- When assisting hygiene, take patient photo, start patient education system, and clean rooms after dismissing patient.
- Set up treatment room, and develop radiographs.
- Seat patients.
- Assist doctor(s) with exams.
- Escort patient to check-out.
- Set up hygiene trays and return to proper operatory.
- Place instruments in the ultrasonic.
- Bag and sterilize instruments.
- Seat patients.

- Have instruments prepared and ready for use.
- Assist, when needed.
- Restock hygiene rooms.
- Place inventory items on list when needed.
- Straighten reception area.
- Check and restock bathrooms in the AM and again in the PM.
- Clean lab and impression trays, and replenish cold sterile.
- Sterilize hygiene hand pieces.
- Assist with sealants.

Chairside Dental Assistant

You will need at least one X-ray-certified dental assistant. If you have only one assistant, it's best to employ someone with a background in expanded duties.

Please delegate to your assistant! Doing so will greatly reduce your stress and allow your assistant to perform duties for which she was trained. *Dentists who do not* allow their certified assistant to make temporary crowns, take impressions, and do numerous other tasks they are trained to do may find themselves with a discouraged Assistant. Many will seek employment in practices that will utilize their skills.

A chairside assistant's main duties are to attend morning huddle, review the schedule for the day, seat patients, and assist doctors during procedures. They should anticipate the needs of patients and see to their comfort, document treatments in patient charts, and update treatment plans.

Other duties include, but are not limited to, the following:

- Upon arrival to work, turn on computers and X-ray programs.

- Run autoclave and Statim.
- Fill and run ultrasonic.
- Set up treatment rooms; stock with trays and supplies, as needed.
- Package lab cases, and make sure they are sent to the appropriate lab.
- Print lab scripts and prescriptions.
- Disinfect, set up, and break down treatment rooms between patients
- Take radiographs as ordered by the doctor.
- Take alginate impressions as ordered by the Doctor.
- Monitor nitrous tanks.
- Keep the lab neat and clean.
- Clean debris from operatory and lab floors, as needed.
- Inform Inventory Coordinator of needed supplies.
- At the end of the day, load autoclave and statim, and empty ultrasonic.
- Turn off computers and X-ray machines.
- Turn off air and vacuum systems.
- Check nitrous tanks, and make sure switches are off.
- Raise chairs and rheostats.

Office Manager

An **office manager** may be necessary for a practice with more than six employees. A true office manager handles financial matters, human resources, marketing, and accounts payable. A written job description is necessary for this position

The office manager's duties include, but are not limited to, the following:

- Maintain employee records.
- Handle accounts payable.
- Hold interviews when positions are available.
- Assist practice owner in making final hiring decisions.
- Make sure necessary documents are filled out, reviewed, and signed by new employees.
- Provide new-employee orientation.
- Make introductions of new employees to existing team members.
- Make sure all employees have clear job descriptions.
- Hold performance reviews, and maintain records of reviews.
- Handle all payroll, and maintain payroll records.
- Maintain records of employee vacation or PTO (paid time off) earned and used.
- Maintain records of employee days missed.
- Maintain records of employee holidays earned and used.
- Maintain records of warnings and disciplinary actions of employees.
- Maintain practice budget.

- Delegate clinical supply inventory control person, and give budget.
- Delegate office supply inventory control person, and give budget.
- Maintain all compliance manuals, and ascertain yearly training and signatures.
- Oversee all heads of department: assistant, hygiene, and business office.
- Report to business owner on a weekly basis or more often, if necessary.
- Oversee and maintain practice overhead goals.
- Facilitate team meetings.

Determining How Many Employees You Need

- Rule of thumb: One front-desk (FD) person is adequate for up to $600,000 in production. Typically, when production reaches more than $600,000 in a one year period, you will need additional help at the front desk. Whether you hire a part-time FD person or have another employee cross-trained and allotted time to work at the front desk, is a decision to be made based on your overhead and overall employee needs.
- You will need one hygiene day for every 225 active patients. When utilizing a hygiene assistant, you will need one assisted hygiene day for every 345 active patients.

For example: If you have 1,200 active patients, you need 5 hygiene days.

1200/225 = 5.33

In this case, you may need a full-time hygienist or two part-time hygienists. Depending on what you consider full time. If four days is full time in your practice, you will need a full time and a part time hygienist. Unless you employee a hygiene assistant.

When utilizing a hygiene assistant for the same number of active patients, you need 3.5 hygiene days.

1200/345 = 3.5

You will likely need a second dental assistant when the Doctor's production reaches $500,000 per year.

Another way to determine whether you need an additional assistant is to look at patient flow. If you're consistently running behind and have a frustrated dental assistant, you should hire a second assist immediately. Whether you hire full-time or part-time, is a decision you should base on the needs of your practice. An assistant can be trained to assist with front-office duties, hygiene patients, handle inventory control and compliance control officer duties.

Personnel Files, Forms and Checklists

Following are forms and a checklist of documents and documentation needed for each new employee. These items should be complete, up to date, and kept in personnel files.

Interviewing a Potential Employee

It's important to have a list of questions for each position and ask the same questions of each candidate for that position. This ensures that you compare apples to apples.

I've included a general sample interview questionnaire here. It is not position specific, it will however, help you get to know a potential employee.

You will want to have a separate questionnaire for each position required in your practice.

Interview Questionnaire

Name: ______________________________

Date: _______________

1. Tell me about yourself.

____

____

____

____

Comments:

____

____

____

____

2. Three characteristics that describe you.

____

____

____

Comments:

____

____

____

3. If you and your former employer had a disagreement, how did you handle it?

Comments:

4. What did you like best about your last (or present) position?

Comments:

5. What did you like least?

Comments:

6. Did you have any special abilities or talents that were never recognized at your last job?

Comments:

7. How would you handle an irate patient on the telephone?

Comments:

8. Discuss some of the problems that you encountered at your last job.

Comments:

9. How many days did you lose from work—for any reason—last year?

Comments:

10. What new skills would you like to learn?

Comments:

11. What kind of people annoy you?

Comments:

12. Why did you leave your past jobs, or what were the circumstances concerning your leaving?

Comments:

13. Describe the best boss you ever had.

Comments:

14. Describe the worst boss you ever had.

Comments:

15. What do you consider to be your greatest strengths?

Comments:

16. What do you consider to be your greatest weaknesses?

Comments:

17. What are your salary needs?

Comments:

18. How much notice would you need to give your current employer?

Comments:

19. Are you under a non-compete, non-solicitation agreement with your current employer? If so, what are the terms?

Comments:

"Unless it's in writing, it wasn't said, it didn't happen and no one knew." ~MFD

Applicant Name: ________________________________

Address: ________________________________

City: ____________________ State: _____Zip: __________

Phone #: ______________

Emergency Contact: ________________________________

Emergency Contact Phone #: ______________________

Position Interviewed for: __________________________

Date Interviewed: ______________________________

Employment Information

Date of Employment: ____________________________

Position Filled: ___________________________

Social Security #: __________________________

Salary/Wages: ___________________________

Per: ________________________________

Hours: ______________________________

FT/PT: ____

Insurance Information: ______________________________

Employee declines group insurance (covered under another policy):

____

Employee Initial: ____________________________________

Date of Insurance Eligibility: ________________________

Coverage Accepted: __________________________________

Effective Date: _______________________________________

Coverage Denied: ____________________________________

Reason: ____

If family coverage, monthly amount to be deducted from payroll:

____

Accounting department notified by: _______________________

Date: ____

New Employee Checklist

(Initial when Completed)

___ Application and/or resume on file

___ Office key given

___ W-4 form

___ I-9 form

___ Instructions given for opening and closing office

___ SS# on file

___ Protocol for tracking hours

___ Insurance application or declination form

___ Security precautions explained

___ Copy of certifications and license on file

___ O.S.H.A. training completed and signature obtained

___ Employment Eligibility Verification (Form I-9)

___ Staff Non-Disclosure explained and signature obtained

___ Personnel Procedure Manual reviewed and employee signature obtained

___ Hepatitis B vaccination:

Confirmation signed OR

___ HIPAA training completed and signature obtained

___ Declination signed

___ Radiation Policy reviewed and signature obtained (where appropriate)

___ Vaccination series started

Performance reviews:

Employee Name: ____

Date: _________

90-Day performance review:

____

____

____

Date: Salary Increase: No Yes Amount: $_________ Total: $____________

6-Month Review:

____

____

Date: Salary Increase: No Yes Amount: $________ Total: $___________

12-Month Review:

____

____

____

____

Date: Salary Increase: No Yes Amount: $________ Total: $___________

Additional Items to Be Kept in Personnel Files

Copy of certifications and licenses

Performance review notes

- Declination or acceptance forms for hepatitis and health insurance coverage
- Hepatitis vaccination forms (treatment record or declination form)
- Incident reports
- Signed non-solicitation forms
- Employment contract
- Compensation package information
- Notes regarding disciplinary action or warnings
- Notes regarding conversations about employment

Personnel Manual

Your employee policy manual should to lay out expectations and policies for your team and let them know what they can expect from you.

If you ever have a labor dispute with an employee, you will be very happy to have this manual. It's the first thing the labor board will ask to see, if you're called before them, due to an employee complaint. The way they see it is, if it's not in writing or there is no employee signature, the employee was not aware of your policy. The ruling will be in favor of the employee.

My personal experience with the Department of Labor.

I was asked by a client to take a call from the Department of Labor regarding a complaint from a former employee of this client. The employee quit her job and started work for another practice closer to her home. She then filed a complaint stating that in her last paycheck she had not been paid for holidays or vacation for the remainder of the year.

My conversation with the interviewer from the Department of Labor went as follows:

The interviewer asked me if the practice owner provided a written personnel manual to employees. I stated that he did. She then asked if there was a section in the manual that outlined the practice policy for payment of vacation and holidays when an employee was terminated or resigned. I was able to say that indeed there was such a policy, and it stated very clearly that both holiday and vacation pay accrue throughout the year. It also went on to say that if an employee voluntarily resigns, they will not be compensated for unearned vacation leave or holiday pay. The employee signed the signature page stating that she had read and understood the manual.

The interviewer asked if I could email the personnel manual to her. I did as she asked and we were notified within a couple of days that the complaint was dismissed. The investigator found that the Personnel manual did clearly spell out the practice policy for holidays and vacations pay. The DOL dismissed the complaint and found in favor of the practice owner.

Determining Pay and Benefits

When determining pay and benefits for your team, familiarize yourself with the going rate of pay in your region for each position in your practice. There are a few websites you can utilize: Salary Wizard, PayScale, Dental Economics®, and Glassdoor are all resources for dental employee wages. You can certainly confer with colleagues as well.

When determining what benefits to offer your team, you must first look at what you can afford, then what's expected and what the market calls for.

Employee benefits may be offered as the practice becomes successful. Benefits to consider are Health Insurance, Retirement, Uniforms, Vacation Days, Holiday Pay and Sick days. Vacation and sick days are often combined as PTO.

All pay increases should be based on merit. You are not required to give an employee a raise because they've remained in your employ another year. Cost of living raises are a different matter. Regardless of how and when you give pay raises, your policy must be clearly spelled out in your employee/personnel manual.

Some things to think about when considering a pay increase:

- Does the employee contribute to your practice in the ways you expect them to?
- Has the employee grown as they should?
- Does the employee come to work on time?
- Does the employee take initiative where appropriate?
- Does the employee stay late without complaining?

Note: Document all pay-increase discussions in the employee's personnel file.

Practice Policies, Protocol and Systems

Sample Reprimand Protocol

To prevent a lawsuit for wrongful discharge, establish a discipline protocol.

Following is a sample reprimand protocol:

1. COUNSELING

Counseling an employee should be the first step in addressing an unsatisfactory performance or attitude of an employee. You should assume that the individual wants to be productive and will correct issues. All counseling should be documented in the personnel file.

2. WRITTEN REPRIMAND

All discussions and discipline should be in writing and should emphasize the importance of the situation, describe the deficiency, review previous discussions, and define the standards of attitude and performance that are expected. A finite amount of time should be given to the employee for compliance.

Lay out consequences that the employee can expect, and give a copy of them to the employee. A copy also should be placed in the employee's personnel file. Set a follow-up date.

3. FINAL WRITTEN WARNING

In giving final warning, you should make it clear that the responsibility for continued employment is in the employee's hands.

A final warning should contain the following:

1. Copies of previous written warnings.
2. Specific areas in which the employee must improve.
3. The period of time employee was given to meet the terms of the final warning.
4. A statement that this is the last opportunity to make the necessary changes required to maintain employment. The next step is termination.

*A copy of the warning should be given to the employee, and one should be placed in the personnel file.

4. DISMISSAL

Obtain the employee's keys, give them their final paycheck or statement, and escort the former employee out of the office.

Practice Policies and Procedures:

Phones

Phones should be answered by or before the third ring. The caller expects to hear a cheerful and confident voice. I recommend that the person who answers the phone, answer with a smile. It's impossible to sound grumpy when you are smiling.

Small dental practices can get away with an answering machine when closed; however, larger practices should consider utilizing an answering service or schedule staggered lunches. Existing and potential patients, often call to schedule an appointment during their lunch break. Having someone answering the phones at the practice will ensure that callers' questions are answered and allow them to schedule an appointment at the same time. An exception to the staggered lunch, should be made, during scheduled team meetings.

While on the phone, a patient should not be placed on "hold" unless you are doing something specifically for the patient. Please do not put the patient on hold to answer the other phone or check a patient in or out. The person on the phone should be given your full attention until you hang up.

Scheduling

When determining the number of doctor and hygiene days needed, you should have 1 doctor day per week per 300 active patients and 1 hygiene day per week per 225 active patients.

Once you have a daily goal set for production, you will want to make sure that procedure codes or codes are placed on the schedule along with the patients' names. This is a good time to use exploding codes, where appropriate. In doing this you enable your software to calculate the amount of production you have scheduled for the day. You can now tweak your schedule to meet production goals.

I am a believer in using your practice management software's daily routing sheet. Even paperless practices should have a routing sheet for each patient. It is the most efficient way to see what's going on with a patient at a glance. Reducing the amount of time it takes to flip from screen to screen.

Scheduling of Dental Procedures

The average amount of time needed for the procedures most often performed.

- Adult prophy = 50 minutes (including exam): Some practice allow 60 minutes for an adult prophy with exam
- Child prophy = 30 to 40 minutes (including exam)
- Sealants = 30 minutes (for first molars) to 1 hour (for entire mouth—all molars and premolars)

- FMX = 20 to 30 minutes
- Panorex = 10 minutes
- Impressions (alginate) = 10 minutes
- RPSC half mouth = 1.5 hours
- Full-mouth debridement = 1 hour
- Perio maintenance = 50 minutes to 1 hour and 10 minutes
- One surface composite = 30 minutes
- Two surface composites = 40 minutes
- Three surface composites = 40 to 50 minutes
- Crown prep, impression, and temporary crown placement = 1.5 hours (single unit)
- Crown prep and delivery with CadCam = 1 to 1.5 hours
- Bridge prep, impression, and temporary = 2 to 2.5 hours.
- Implant restoration = 45 minutes to 1 hour
- Anterior root canal = 1 hour
- Premolar root canal = 1.5 hours
- Molar root canal = 1.5 to 2 hours

Confirmation of benefits:

Dental insurance benefits are not as easy for a patient to ascertain as health insurance benefits. Patients often need help determining coverage. The internet gives us the ability to confirm benefits in a more efficient way. As more practices take advantage of the internet, the days of holding 'for the next available agent' are quickly becoming a thing of the past.

Insurance claims should be sent daily, at the very least. Some practices send claims after each patient, some file claims before lunch and again at the end of the day. Utilizing electronic claims submission software is an absolute must. There are insurance companies that will no longer accept paper claims.

When filing insurance claims, radiographs are required for the following procedures: Periodontal root planing and scaling (will also require periodontal charting and possible narrative), Full mouth debridement, Endodontic procedures, Crown and bridge procedures and Orthodontic treatment. There are circumstances in which other procedures will require a radiograph as well, it is dependent on the insurance claim reviewer and provider.

Standard of Care

It's essential that you establish a standard of care for your entire team to follow. It must be uniform throughout the practice, with everyone on the same page. This will prevent misunderstandings between staff members, doctor and staff, and staff and patients.

Example: If you believe a tooth with a three surface filling should be crowned if recurrent decay is found, stick with that decision, it is your standard of care. What you don't want to do is tell Mrs. Smith, who presents with a three surface filling and recurrent decay, that you can "watch" the tooth and tell Mrs. Jones, who has the same issue, that the tooth should be crowned. There is no better way to confuse your team and make them afraid to take initiative. Cohesive teams have leaders who are consistent in all areas of their business.

If a patient refuses treatment after receiving your diagnosis and professional opinion regarding the best course of treatment, that's their decision. Your assistant or hygienist must document your diagnosis and your recommendation for treatment. It is perfectly acceptable to mention a less desirable course of treatment, after you have advised as to the best course of treatment.

Financial Policies:

All financial policies should be in writing and included in new patient registration forms.

Cancellation policy:

Make sure there is a place for a patient signature on your written cancellation policy.

Policy example: One broken appointment or short notice cancellation with an excuse and the patient may reschedule at their convenience. If there is a second broken appointment or short notice cancellation it suggests that the patient is unable to commit to an appointment. This patient should be placed on a short notice call list to be called when you have an opening.

Policy for Patient Insurance Claims

Patients should be provided with your practice insurance policy. It should be included in the new-patient information packet. Make sure the policy is clear, and require a signature.

Details of your policy will be determined by your level of involvement with dental insurance companies and whether you are a participating provider or file insurance as a courtesy only.

About Your Team

Training

First and foremost, don't skimp on training for your team. If you do, it will cost your practice many times more than the training would have cost. In addition, don't assume know everything they need to know.

- Your team will need ongoing training to fully utilize the practice management software.
- Dental teams require ongoing training to keep up with what's going on in the insurance industry and make changes in protocol and coding as needed. Coding, procedures, coverage and filing requirements are ever changing. If you file insurance on behalf of your patients, you will lose money if your team is not on top of these changes. If you send only one team member for outside training, schedule a training meeting with the remainder of your team as soon as possible. Your entire team should be aware of changes in any system affecting your patients.
- In limiting team training, you put yourself at risk for large fines and the possibility losing of your license for failure to comply with government regulations. I've seen this scenario happen multiple times.
- Job satisfaction rates are higher for well-trained employees. You will reap benefits that outweigh the expense of training many times over.

The story of an employee who thought she knew and told her employers she knew, but she REALLY didn't know!

While visiting a new practice, and performing a practice assessment, I discovered 69 pages of outstanding insurance claims totaling over 100,000.00. The practice owner had no idea.

It took just a little digging to find that the person in charge of insurance claims, followed up, only when a request was received for more information on a claim. She was not trained to follow up on Insurance claims that were not paid in 30 days. She had no idea how to do it or who to call and didn't even realize that an outstanding insurance claims report existed.

This practice utilizes practice management software that does not age an account until the insurance claim is closed. There were hundreds of patients who owed money to the practice and had no idea.

With training, they worked through the claims, received payment on what was covered, and billed patients for their portion. They now utilize the internet and their Practice Management Software to confirm benefits, check on claim status and refile claims as needed.

Having a back log of unpaid insurance claims led to another issue: Patients didn't understand why they received bills for services rendered several months or even a year prior. Claims older than a year were written off. Not fun!

Having one employee who claimed to be proficient at 'handling' dental insurance caused a huge snowball effect of problems for this practice. One system failure leads to another, and they all lead to loss in revenue for the practice.

"Assuming an employee has the proper training needed to manage important areas of your practice, can be a costly mistake." ~MFD

Additional Tips for Training and Continuity.

Following these recommendations will hasten new employee training.

- Take photos of a tray set-up for each procedure.
- Take photos of treatment rooms, after they have been closed for the day.
- Take pictures of the lab, clean, neat, and the way it should look at the end of each work day.
- Take pictures of the sterilization area the way it should look at the end of each work day.
- Take pictures of all areas and equipment that need to be cleaned and maintained, with instructions on how to do it.

Place photos in a binder or inside a cabinet door in appropriate locations.

True Story of a Dentist with a "Golf habit"?

A dentist wanted to take the afternoon off to play golf and mentioned it to his Scheduling Coordinator. She reminded him that he had taken a lot of time off lately and she had asked some patients to reschedule several times.

She suggested that she shouldn't move them again because they may leave the practice.

This dentist completely lost his cool and stormed back to his office. In a few minutes, he returned with a roll of duct tape and proceeded to duct tape the phone to her head, before she even realized what he was doing. He looked at her and said, "I'm the boss here, I pay your salary. Call those ___ patients and reschedule!"

The doctor had labor board, peer review, state board and a few other issues to deal with following this incident.

Walk out before you lose your cool! ;-)

Team Communication

Morning Huddle

The most important communication of the day is your morning huddle. If you don't have another meeting with your team, you should have this one. This 10 to 15-minute team meeting, prior to seeing the first patient of the day, is essential. It provides time for you, as a team, to look ahead at the day and eliminate many of the little problems that occur throughout the day. This meeting sets the tone for your day.

Eliminating problems before they occur provides for more efficient, productive, profitable and stress-free days.

Your Morning Huddle is not the appropriate time to bring up staff issues, unless they absolutely cannot wait until the next regular team meeting.

See Sample Morning Huddle Sheet on next page:

Facilitator: To Do Before Morning Huddle

- ☐ Provide a copy of the day's schedule to all staff members.
- ☐ Keep the telephone answering machine/service on until after the meeting.
- ☐ Gather information of interest with regards to the day's patients, such as birthdays, engagements, marriage, new babies, etc.

Office manager, office coordinator, or scheduling coordinator

- ☐ Start meeting on time.
- ☐ Discuss each patient, allowing the clinician and appointment coordinator to elaborate, as needed.

Assistant (Prior to morning huddle)

- ☐ Review schedule and treatment for each patient.

Assistant (During huddle)

- ☐ Discuss, as needed, today's schedule and time needed for treatments.
- ☐ Discuss patients in need of pre-med or nitrous.

Hygienist (Prior to morning huddle)

- ☐ Review the schedule and patient charts for the day.
- ☐ Note previously diagnosed but incomplete treatments.

Hygienist (During huddle)

- ☐ Advise as to previously diagnosed but incomplete treatment of scheduled patients.
- ☐ Review doctor schedule for openings for patients in need of treatment.

Appointment Coordinator

- ☐ Advise of new patients, review new patient information, ascertain best placement for emergency patients, and review changes in schedule to source treatment.

Financial Coordinator

- ☐ Reaffirm the goal amounts for production ($_) and collection ($__). Discuss how you're progressing towards those goals.
- ☐ Discuss any additional comments concerning today's schedule.
- ☐ Close the meeting on time and on a positive note.

Team Meetings

It's important to have regular team meetings to keep your team motivated and on board with practice goals. Team meetings are the time to address housekeeping issues.

I recommend that practices with fewer than five team members meet for a minimum of two hours every other month. Teams of six or more should meet every month for a minimum of two hours. Have a meeting agenda, and try to stick to it. Leave time for a question-and-answer period at the end of the meeting.

Order in or bring lunch, lock the office door, and place a note on the door stating that the office will be closed until __ o'clock.

The meeting should be held in a quiet place where interruptions will not be an issue. The office phone should be turned over to the answering service, and every employee should be in attendance. Always start and end team meetings on a positive note.

Team Incentive Bonuses

I'm a huge advocate of incentive plans and believe that, when done correctly, they can be fair to the practice owner and the employees, as well as being a wonderful benefit and a morale-builder.

The plan I recommend meets this standard. The team splits 20% of anything over a set goal, and the practice/dentist/practice owner receives the remaining 80%.

The 20% that the team receives is divided between team members based on the number of days worked in the goal period. By rewarding those who pick up the slack when someone is out sick or on vacation, you incentivize your team members to go the extra mile.

I believe that a monthly incentive goal provides consistent motivation, whereas quarterly or yearly goals are mostly, out of sight and out of mind.

How an Incentive Bonus made a big difference!

A few years ago, I coached in a practice with 2 dental hygienists producing an average of $825 per day. After running a practice potential analysis, as I do with all practices, I found that based on the practice fee schedule, the number of patient hours available per day, the number of active patients, number of patient days available per week and number of weeks worked per year, the hygiene department was capable of producing several hundred dollars more per day and $120,000 more per year.

We worked with the hygiene team and shared tools and resources to make the most of each patient appointment. We offered an incentive bonus of 20% of any dollar amount they produced above their goal on a monthly basis. We set the goal based on 85% of their daily potential, based on the practice potential analysis report. They were supplied with daily and weekly monitors to keep track of patients, procedures, and production. We asked them to try it our way for three months.

I reviewed the practice analysis report with the hygiene team and shared with them—realistically—what the hygiene department should be producing. It was decided that a periodontal treatment program would be implemented. Training was provided.

In the first month hygiene production went from $825 per day to $990 per day. In the second month, hygiene production rose to $1,050 per day, and by the third month, they were producing $1,175 per day on average. The hygienists began making major bonuses prior to completely implementing the periodontal program. Once the program was completely implemented, patient appointment times were maximized and the hygiene department became a profit center for the practice.

The goal was increased at the end of three months, as discussed. The practice settled on a protocol that worked well with the practice philosophy and standard of care. The hygiene department was re-energized, and the practice had a new energy about it.

Hygiene Production Goals: Hygiene daily goals should be determined by your fee schedule and the number patient hours available each day. As a rule, 50% of hygiene patients will need BWX, 1/3 of hygiene patients will need a panoramic X-ray or FMX and, on average, 1 perio SRP or perio maintenance per day. To determine the percentage of child prophy appointments necessary, review the patient analysis report to see the patient mix. Incorporate as indicated by the numbers. If this report is not available; a good rule of thumb is ¼ to 1/3 of a general dental practice patient base consists of children. You will likely have a good feel as to which percentage to use.

Hygiene bonus systems are typically based on a production goal and are often separate from the incentive plans of the administrative and auxiliary teams.

You may set the hygiene daily goal, as defined above or you may want to use the rule of thumb that hygienists should produce at minimum of 3 times their compensation rate. When using hygiene compensation rate to determine daily goal; the compensation rate utilized, should include wages and benefits, sans prior bonus plan (if applicable).

Credit for the exam should go to the dentist.

When setting a monthly goal, you start with your daily goal and multiply it by the number of days the hygienists works in the month.

See Below:

Example Hygiene Incentive Bonus: Daily goal = $1,000 Number of days worked in the month = 16 Goal: 16 x 1,000 = 16,000 Actual production was 18,000 18,000 prod. - 16,000 goal = 2,000 over goal 2,000 x 0.20 = 400.00 is the amount of hygiene bonus for the month

Keep in mind, 80% of the amount over the monthly goal goes back to the practice or to the practice owner.

Incentive Bonus for Administrative and Auxiliary Team Members.

Steps in Determining your Goal.

First, you must know the total cost to run your practice on a monthly basis. Take your total practice expenses for the last 12 months, and divide them by 12. This will give you a good starting point.

If you're not sure what your total practice expenses are, ask your accountant. If the practice owner receives a salary, it should be added to the total practice expenses when setting the goal.

It's important that the goal be achievable and that it not be raised for a minimum of three months. When you raise it, do it in a way that makes sense, and discuss it ahead of time with your team.

When implementing the bonus system for your administrative and auxiliary team, you will set your monthly goal based on collections. They will bonus 20% of any $ amount collected over the goal. The bonus amount will be paid based on the number of days they worked in the month bonused.

The total number of days worked by all employees divided into the bonus amount will give you the total $ bonus per day. You then multiply the daily amount by the number of days each employee worked, to get their individual bonus amount.

*Note: If you have a separate bonus system set up for the hygiene department, their days will be counted in the total of employee work days, but they will not be paid a bonus on collections. In this case, hygienists have their own bonus based on production.

Example:

Monthly goal = 100,000.00

Actual Collections = 120,000.00

120,000.00 collections – 100,000.00 goal = 20,000 over goal

20,000 x 0.20 = 4,000.00 bonus amount

Team Member~# of Days worked~Daily bonus~Total bonus

Susan Admin	15	X	47.05	705.75
Amy Admin	15	X	47.05	705.75
Glenda Asst.	15	X	47.05	705.75
Cindy Asst.	15	X	47.05	705.75
Denise Hyg.	15	(Separate Bonus system)		
Linda Hyg.	10	(Separate Bonus system)		

Total days worked by all team members = 85

Bonus amount = 4,000.00 /85 days = 47.05 bonus per work day.

Remember: 80% of collections, over the goal, stays with the practice/owner.

The Patient Experience

What do patients see when they walk in to your office?

It's important that you and your team enter the office from the patient entrance on a regular basis. You need to see what your patients see, when they enter your practice. Check for dirty entrance ways, cobwebs, faded signs and trash. Also, look at the décor as you walk in the door. Is it inviting and comfortable? Keep in mind, you're not just looking through the eyes of current patients. Look through the eyes of new patients too. Ask team members for their opinions and please consider taking their advice. Simple, inexpensive updates can make a huge difference in the look and feel of a practice.

Patients should be greeted with a smile within a few seconds of walking in the door and should be made to feel as if they are the most important patient of the day.

New Patients

You have one chance, and only one, to make a first impression. Whether it's the way your phones are answered or how the patient is greeted when they enter the office, it is essential that every new patient feel appreciated.

When engaging with any patient, it is imperative that you listen to them, sit at their level and look them in the eye (Please, don't stand above and speak down to patients). Encourage them to ask questions. A great way to end your first meeting with a patient is to say something along the lines of "It was a pleasure to meet you. Thanks for coming in to see us and we look forward to seeing you next time."

Follow up with a new-patient thank-you letter. It's a very simple, yet meaningful way to let the patient know they are appreciated. The letter should thank the patient for trusting you with their dental care and should welcome a call should they have a question. It should be signed by the doctor and every team member. I recommend that new patient letters be signed during the morning huddle. A hand-signed letter is impressive and will be much appreciated.

Patient Registration

Use online forms for patient convenience. You should have a tab on your website and a page for patient registration forms. Included, should be forms for patient health history, insurance information and policy, your financial policies, HIPAA forms, your cancellation policy, and any other forms you want to share with new patients.

Patient Communication

Whether by phone, text or email, it's important to stay in touch with your patients.

Patient Communication Systems

I am a big fan of utilizing a patient communication system that integrates with practice management software. There are several available. Examples: Demandforce, Solutionreach, Revenue Well, Practice Mojo, Weave, and Lighthouse 360. Ask your dental supply rep or consultant for a recommendation. There are huge benefits to using patient communications software.

People are busier today than ever and rarely find it convenient to take a confirmation phone call at work. Therefore reminding patients of their appointment via text or email and allowing them to confirm in kind, is much preferred. Patients love this option and appreciate the ability to communicate with your office electronically.

Other ways to utilize Patient Communication Software:

- Send emails or texts for overdue hygiene appointments.
- Send emails or texts to patients who have missed an appointment. Remind them of the importance of their dental care and how it affects overall health.
- Send Holiday greetings.
- Send Happy Birthday" texts or emails.
- Send notification of promotions or special offers.
- Send a practice bulletin or newsletter.

Treatment Financing Options

Dentists are direct dental care providers and should never discuss treatment fees with a patient. Don't confuse your roll in the eyes of your patient. The office or financial coordinator should handle all discussions involving cost of treatment and payment options.

In-Office Financing

Many dental practices offer in-office financing. If you choose to go this route, you must put all arrangements in writing. You may want to perform a credit check, and you should charge interest as well.

In-Office Dental Care Plans

An in office dental care plan is an option that allows patients, without dental insurance, to receive dental care at discounted rate. Note: The patient will pay a fee to become a member of your plan and all treatment, outside of the plan, is paid 100% by the patient at time of treatment. See some examples below.

EXAMPLE:

In-Office Dental Plan

A membership plan in which patients pay an annual fee and receive basic dental treatment during their membership period. Members also receive a discounted percentage (15-25% is the average) off of the normal fee for most dental procedures, not included in the plan. There are exclusions.

BENEFITS:

- No annual deductible and no annual maximum
- 2 PERIODIC EXAMS PER YEAR
- ADULT OR CHILD PROPHY 2 times PER YEAR
  2 FLOURIDE TREATMENTS PER YEAR with a child prophy
- 2 OR 4 BITEWING RADIOGRAPHS PER YEAR
- __% DISCOUNT ON MOST DENTAL TREATMENT COMPLETED WITHIN 12 MONTHS
  OF ENROLLMENT when PAID IN FULL AT TIME OF SERVICE. Exclusions include implants and Invisalign/clear correct/6 month braces.
- ANNUAL Fee:
- Individual patient fee $__ per year (example 335.00)
- Additional Family Members $__ per person (example 250.00)

Must pay balance in full when services are rendered to receive discounted fee.

NO REFUNDS will be GIVEN IF PATIENT Chooses not to take advantage of DENTAL membership PLAN benefits

For those who prefer to offer membership levels, I have included some examples below:

Level I

Exam: Two times per year

Bitewing X-rays: One time per year

Simple prophy: Two times per year, adult or child

Fluoride treatment 2 times per year for children

Fee: $ Practice sets this fee. Example would be 295.00.

Level II

Includes level I benefits plus:

- A panoramic radiograph or a full mouth series
- 25% discount on simple restorations (does not include crown and Bridge, full or partial dentures, root canal therapy, Invisalign or implants.
- Fee: You set your fee. Example would be 495.00.

Level III

- Includes all Levels I and II benefits plus:
- Full mouth Perio scaling and root planning to replace prophy
- Perio maintenance appointment to replace prophy
- Fee: You set your fee. Example would be 1.495.00

Third-Party Financing Options

CareCredit® has been around a long time. They offer competitive rates and have several plans from which to choose.

There are other third-party finance options. Ask colleagues or visit with providers exhibiting during a dental conference.

Fee Schedule

Obtaining a fee schedule comparison is as easy as making a call to your dental supply representative. Large dental supply companies offer a practice analysis report detailing where your fees fall in comparison with other practices in your area.

Several dental-specific magazines publish fee schedule surveys each year.

Note: Your fee schedule should be balanced annually, otherwise you leave tens of thousands of dollars on the table each year.

"Charge what you're worth and be worth what you charge."
~Unknown

Risk Management

Compliance

Dental practices are required to have, within the practice, a compliance officer. This team member will coordinate all yearly training sessions and ensure that manuals, training and signature forms are complete and up-to-date.

Note: All compliance manuals require yearly signatures.

OSHA

You will need:

- An OSHA manual with an infection control plan- This manual must be customized to your practice. It must contain training records, dates and signatures of past and current employees.
- A Fire escape protocol. Map and plan
- Incident report protocol with required and up to date forms

You will also need a method of storing MSDS sheets. You can do this via hardcopy, in a notebook, or digital file stored on an office server or cloud based program. The information must be readily available and employees must know how to access the information.

HIPAA

- Your HIPAA manual must be customized to your practice.
- Team members must receive training on your HIPAA policies and protocol prior to or during their first day of

employment. You must have current year signatures from each team member stating that they understand your practice HIPAA policy and protocol and agree to abide by it.

- Your HIPAA policy must be reviewed by your team yearly and updated as needed.

Radiation Safety Manual

- The Radiation safety manual contains federal and state laws as they pertain to radiation exposure and radiographs taken in the dental office.
- It must be customized to your practice.
- Signatures of Employees who take X-rays are required. They must be certified and review practice compliance rules and updates yearly.

Top Causes of Dental Malpractice Lawsuits

Failure to Diagnose Oral Cancer in Early Stages

- Make patients aware that you are performing an oral cancer screening. Talk them through it, discuss findings and Document, Document, Document.

Failure to Diagnose and Treat Periodontal Disease and Failure to Obtain Signatures for Consent or Refusal of Treatment go hand in hand.

- Informed consent forms are both educational and necessary for your practice. Whether treatment refusal forms will always hold up in court is a matter of differing opinions. However, failure to require a signature on the appropriate treatment form, when a patient refuses your diagnoses and recommended treatment, may put your practice and license at risk. Continuing to provide treatment for a patient who refuses treatment and refuses to sign a declination form is certainly not advisable.

- Important: Explain each procedure, obtain consent, render treatment, and document all.
- Explain the need for X-rays, document and discuss diagnosis with the patient.

Following this protocol could mean the difference between winning or losing a malpractice suit.

Patient Abandonment

- Before losing an unhappy patient, every effort should be made to communicate with the patient. Document attempts to communicate and any discussions that follow.
- When dismissing a patient, it is important to know the rules, of your state, regarding patient dismissal and emergency treatment. Check with your state board if you're unsure.

Failure to Refer to a Specialist

- When performing a procedure that would normally be performed by a specialist, you will be held to the same standard of care as the specialist. Be aware of your limits, and form a good relationship with specialists in your area.

Failure to thoroughly Explain Treatment

- Explaining a procedure to a patient should be done face-to-face or knee-to-knee and in a clear, concise manner.
- Listen to the patient's concerns.
- Thoroughly document the conversation.

Detecting Embezzlement

Experts believe that between 50 and 60 percent of dental practice owners will be victims of embezzlement during their career. With the average theft amount of 150,000.00 - 200,000.00, and far too many exceed the 1,000,000.00 mark.

Unfortunately, experts have found that most who embezzle from dental practices are long term employees, entrusted with handling practice finances.

Behaviors and patterns to look for:

- An administrative employee that is very reluctant to train another employee for their position. This person will make excuses as to why no one else can or should be entrusted with their position.
- Rarely takes time away from work.
- Only takes vacation when the doctor is away from the practice.
- Advises his/her fill-in to leave all posting of insurance checks for their return (making it look like they are doing the fill-in a favor).
- Becomes upset at the thought of working with a practice consultant and drags his/her feet at supplying reports.
- Complains to employer about anyone who asks questions with the goal of having the person fired.
- Consistently works late.
- Has a higher standard of living than one would expect.

Details to check in your practice reports;

- Excessive write offs of accounts receivable
- Miscellaneous category in adjustment report with vague explanations for write offs or adjustments.

- Low collection rate when compared with adjusted production.
- Duplicate payments
- Multiple refund checks to one insurance company on a regular basis.

Tips to prevent embezzlement:

- Practice financial systems should be reviewed regularly but, at unexpected times.
- Keep your practice check book and QuickBooks under your supervision.
- Hire a dental specific CPA that provides monthly reports.
- If you suspect embezzlement, hire a fraud detection agency. I recommend David Harris' group.

Forming an Exit Strategy

Hiring an Associate:

If you believe your practice needs an additional dentist, do your research and some soul searching before you begin speaking with potential candidates.

Some things to think about:

- Why do you need an associate?
- Are you busy enough for two doctors full time, part time?
- Are you seeing more than 30 new patients per month?
- Do you have enough treatment rooms?
- Will you be working less hours or the same?
- Do you have the energy to bring an Associate dentist on board with your practice philosophy and standard of care? This will require some teaching on your part.
- Can you afford to take an initial cut in pay?
- Will you need additional staff members to support another dentist? Do you want to hire additional staff?
- What is your timeline?
- Have you had a professional valuation in the past year or two? If not, you should, prior to hiring an Associate dentist.

Once you have made the decision to hire an Associate, there are other considerations to be made.

- Who will provide the employment contract?
- What will the terms of the restrictive covenant be? Is a restrictive covenant enforceable in your state?

- Will you classify the Associate dentist as an employee or an Independent contractor? If the Associate dentist works in a space that you provide, with instruments, supplies and staff you provide, you should consider the Associate an employee. Doing otherwise may set you up for an audit. If the IRS finds the Associate was mis-categorized as an Independent Consultant, you will be required to pay all back taxes and penalties.
- Who will pay for the malpractice insurance?
- Will you offer benefits? CE, Uniforms, Health Insurance.
- How much time off will be allowed? How much notice required for vacation?
- How will you compensate the Associate dentist? Will you pay a percentage of collections or production? What percentage? Will you offer an initial salary or draw?
- How will patients be distributed?
- Who will pay lab fees?
- Who are hygiene checks/exams determined? Please compensate the Associate dentist for the exam.
- Will there be on option to purchase in the future? If so, what are the terms?
- What are the terms of terminating your relationship? How much notice do you require and want to give should either party determine that the relationship is not working? Somewhere between 30 and 90 days is the average.

The Importance of an Exit Strategy

If you are a dental practice owner, you should have an exit strategy in place within a very short time of purchasing a practice. One never knows what tomorrow will bring. As I write this, I have just learned of the crash of a small plane carrying six people. Four of the six were dentists and two other victims were dental spouses. Between them they had 11 children who are now Orphans. I immediately wondered if they planned ahead, if they had practice valuations and letters of instructions for handling their practices and estates.

Your family should be made aware of your wishes and be instructed on how to handle the disposition of your dental practice should something unforeseen happen to you. There is a small window of time to sell a practice following a tragedy such as this. The value of a dental practice falls 5-10% each week following the death of the dentist.

Letter of Instruction

A letter of instruction should contain the names and contact information of those you trust to handle the disposition of your practice. It's advisable to have at least three copies. You should entrust one to your attorney, have one in your safe and give one to a reliable and trust worthy person within your family or very close circle of friends.

Other essential contact names and information included should be that of your:

- Insurance broker
- CPA
- Attorney
- Dental merchandise sales rep
- A designated employee
- Transition consultant/broker
- List of employee names, positions, and contact information.
- Insurance type and policy numbers.

- Important log-in IDs, passwords, account numbers, and contact information.

Practice Valuation

You should have a baseline practice valuation as early as three years into practice ownership.

If you are many years away from retirement, leading transition brokers recommend updating your practice valuation every three years, unless there is a significant change in practice revenue, in which case you should update the valuation yearly. When you are within seven years of retirement, have your valuation updated yearly.

Hiring a professional practice transition company to perform the comprehensive valuation will be one of the best investments you make during your career. Enabling you to better plan for your retirement. Many view their practice valuation as an additional disability or life insurance policy.

Advise your spouse of the location of the valuation. Share a pdf of your valuation with your Accountant. Keep in mind the practice valuator will have the valuation as well. Whether it's located in a digital file or in a safe, make sure it's easily accessible.

What Determines the Value of Your Practice?

If you don't know the answer to this question, you are not alone. Very few dental practice owners have an idea of the value of their practice and have little knowledge of what criteria is used when determining the value.

Important criteria for a dental practice valuation:

- Financial statements and profit and loss for a minimum of three years

- Adjusted net earnings
- True practice overhead
- Number of active patients
- Practice production and collection history for a minimum of three years
- Productivity by procedure and provider report for the previous year or most recent 12 months, depending on the time frame being used.
- Hygiene department productivity percentage
- Copy of current lease (if applicable) or amount required for rent (if owned)
- Recall review (number of patients seen on recall in the last year)
- Equipment: Historical Depreciation schedule. Can parts be purchased to repair equipment if broken?
- Leasehold improvements
- Number of days patients were seen each year, for the past three years
- Year-to-date, aged, accounts receivable report
- A current fee schedule: A buyer will want to know; When was it last updated? How often has it been updated in the past?
- Census of all employees (compensation, benefits, hours worked, positions, responsibilities, and number of years with the practice)
- Average number of new patients per month for the past 12 months
- Insurance policies and premium amounts
- A copy of the non-compete for an associate (if applicable)

Other factors that play a part in determining the value of your practice:

- Practice potential
- Desirability of location
- Revenue source (fee for service, PPO, managed care, Medicaid, clinic)

A dental practice valuation is a subjective opinion based on practice data and the expert opinion of experienced valuators.

You have spent your life building your practice. You deserve to get the most out of it.

Recommended Resources

Social Media

Visit www.LivvieMatthews.com for an online marketing business coach who helps entrepreneurs navigate the digital world of online marketing. Or email Livvie@livviematthews.com.

Website Design, Hosting, and Maintenance

Todd Day Graphics at www.todddaygraphics.com.

Fraud and Embezzlement:

Prosperident is the world's largest firm specializing in the investigation of embezzlement committed against general dentists and dental specialists. This team of experienced fraud examiners, is ideal for investigating suspected or confirmed embezzlement, and for ensuring that office procedures are in place to defend against future embezzlement. Prosperident's website is www.dentalembezzlement.com, and its phone number is 888-398-2327.

Acknowledgements

Please allow me to acknowledge a few people who are very important in my life and career.

To my husband, Todd: Thank you for being my biggest cheerleader, for putting up with the long hours and for your endless support and love. I love you today, tomorrow, and always.

To my daughter, Jamie: Thank you for giving me a reason to work, grow, and learn through some very tough years. Since the day you were born, you were my number one reason "why." I love you so much. Thanks for making me a mom.

To my parents: The reasons I have to thank you are much too long to list, so I'll just say, thank you for giving me a safe and loving place to call home. Thanks for helping me believe in myself, instilling in me a good work ethic, and showing me how important it is to give back. I love you both more than you will ever know.

To my brothers and sister, Steve, Laurence, and Debbie: There aren't words to express the amount of respect I have for each of you. I've watched with awe as you've been so very successful in your careers and personal lives. You've given me a lot to look up to. I hope you know how very proud I am to call you my brothers and sister and I love you all very much!

To Amanda, Betsy, and Mike: Thank you for loving my siblings and my parents. Thank you, too, for my wonderful nieces and nephews. I am one proud aunt, and I love you all.

To my sweet mother-in-law, Ernestine: Thank you for being such a positive and understanding example of love. I hope you know how very important you are to me and that I am so grateful to have you in my life. I love you.

To my friends: Thank you for being supportive during this very busy time in my career, and thank you for understanding and not giving up on me when I'm unable to attend events or gatherings.

To colleagues who have been or are a great influence in my career: Thank you for your friendship and support through the years. You know who you are.

This book is dedicated to all of you!

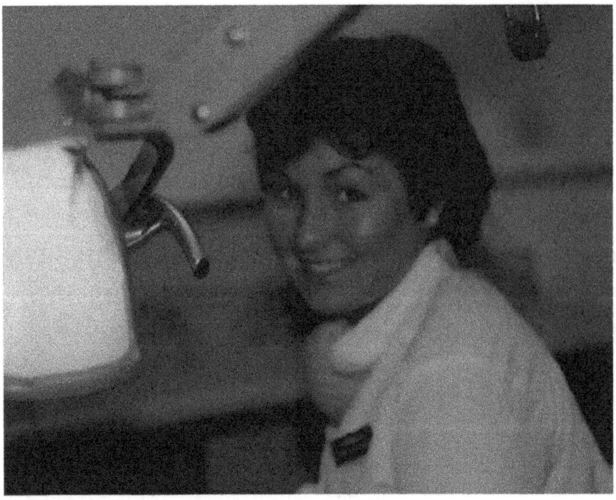

How in the heck did I get here?

I grew up in a small town in South Carolina. My first "job" was babysitting for the little boy of our family dentist and his wife, who were friends of my parents and attended the same church as my family.

On a couple of occasions, my parents needed to go out of town during the school year and this nice couple was left in charge of me (a teenage girl). Yikes! They deserved a medal for taking that on! They truly are the sweetest couple. I always have and always will think the world of them.

All of that said, I hated going to the dentist! I won't even pretend otherwise. When confirmation calls came in for dental appointments, I sometimes “forgot” to give the messages to my Mom. As it turned out, she was always a step ahead of me and made sure I was there at the appointed times.

Although I didn’t enjoy having dental treatment, my dentist was very kind, as was his hygienist. He and his team seemed to have fun at work. Go figure! It was his ability to be funny and kind and her ability to be patient and compassionate while treating a pain in a pain in the butt teenager(me), that lead me to be interested in dentistry.

I shadowed my dentist and his team some while in high school. I enjoyed being on the other side of the chair. So, I graduated from high school a year early, because I could, and started dental assisting school before my high school classmates started their senior year in high school. It was hard! I missed my friends and my parents and my hometown.

I was the youngest person in my dental assisting class. I didn't study much in high school. Microbiology, head and neck anatomy and radiology changed that! I was forced to develop good study habits. I had no intention of failing!

My education included several weeks of training at The Medical University of South Carolina. We lived in old dorms on the MUSC campus with no air conditioning in the middle of the summer.

As a college student, I had very little money, and what I had was used for uniforms and equipment requirements. I remember having $1.50 per day for food while in school at MUSC. I didn't tell my parents; I was stubborn and determined to get by with what I had. Those were lean times, but I'm convinced they helped to build the work ethic I have today.

The year I graduated from dental assisting school, my dentist was president of the local dental society and attended our awards ceremony. I had no idea that I would be presented with the award for Outstanding Clinical Performance, and my dentist was there to present it. That was special! Before the night ended, I would receive another amazing honor. My classmates voted me, the recipient of our Class Merit Award. I remember feeling incredibly honored, a little embarrassed and was very happy that my parents and my dentist were there to witness a very special night.

Here I am more than thirty years later. I still love dentistry and feel blessed to have a career I love.

My hope is that what I've shared in this book will be of help to someone else who loves dentistry.

All my best,

Mary

Facebook: www.facebook.com/Thedentalbusiness/

Twitter: @TheDentalBiz

Linkedin: www.linkedin.com/company/5186022